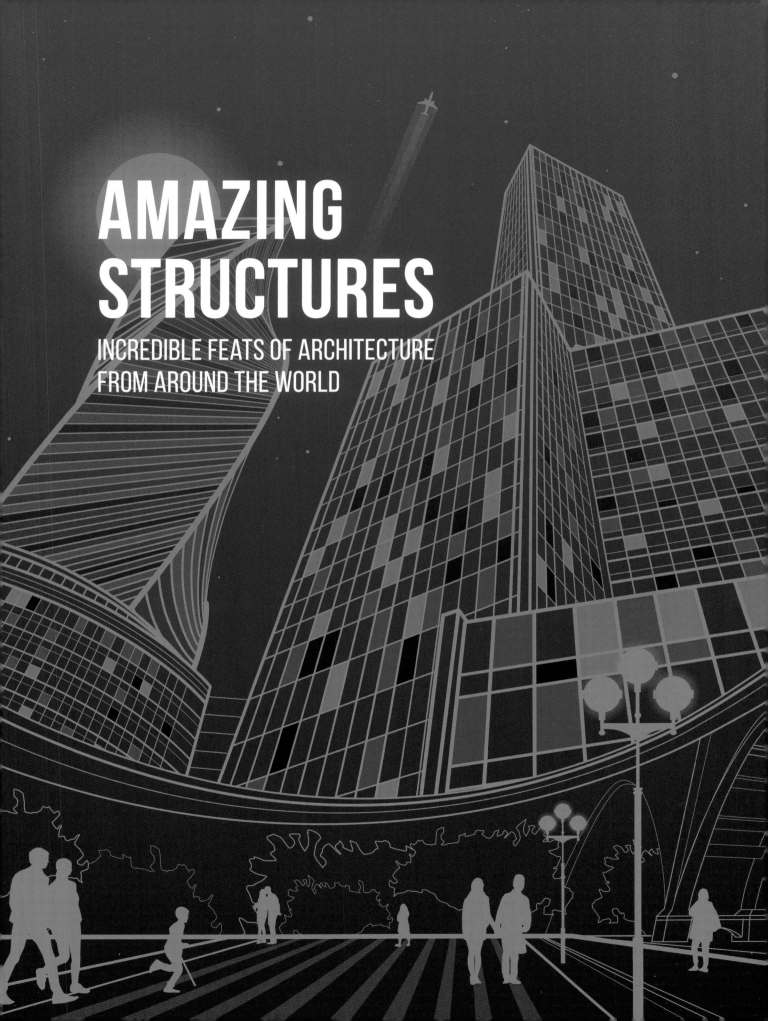

AMAZING STRUCTURES

INCREDIBLE FEATS OF ARCHITECTURE
FROM AROUND THE WORLD

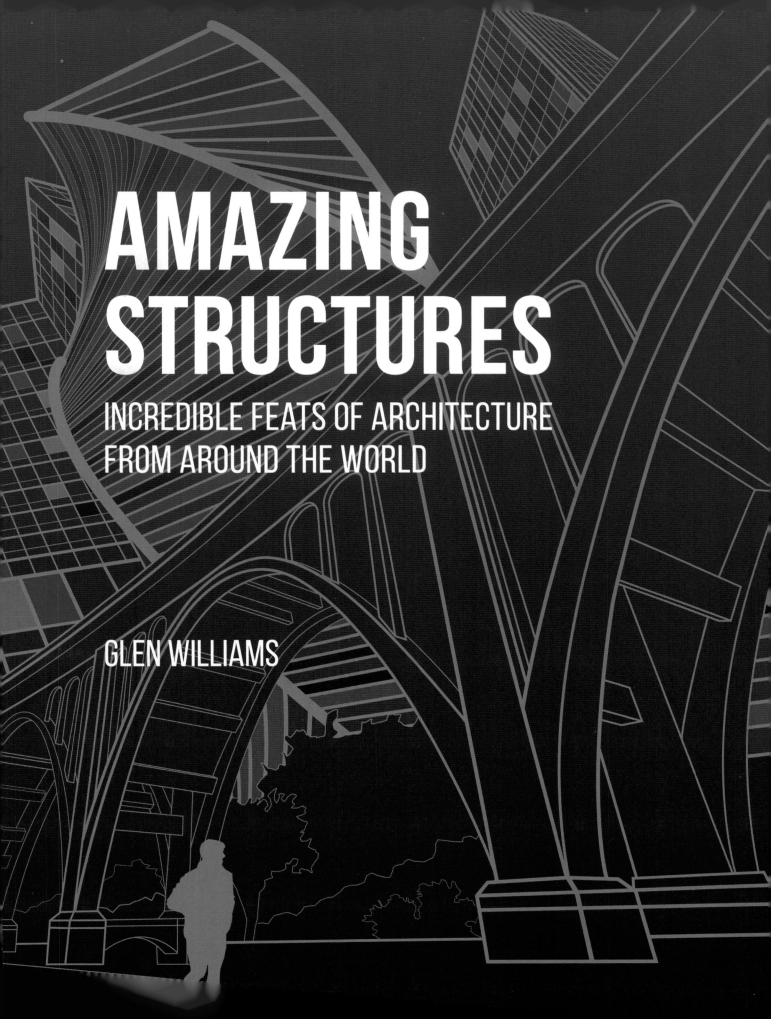

AMAZING STRUCTURES

INCREDIBLE FEATS OF ARCHITECTURE
FROM AROUND THE WORLD

GLEN WILLIAMS

Contents

Introduction

They are the buildings that cause wonder, the structures that speak to us, stir our imaginations and keep us darkening their inspired doorways.

They are not just buildings, they are art. Yes, amazing structures should be soundly built and stable. They should serve the users' needs, to borrow that well-trotted out phrase: 'form follows function'. But we should also throw in a few more 'F words': amazing structures also need to be Fab, Fantastic and Fun.

Ancient, modern and everywhere in between, *Amazing Structures of the World* sets out to explore some much-loved buildings and the stories of how they came to be part of our lives.

Along with many classics, we also pay homage to the new breed of amazing structures – including one so new, it is still on the drawing board.

This book is not only a tribute to some pretty incredible and magical structures, this is also a nod to the architects, the builders (often slave laborers in the classical world), the artisans and the dreamers who pooled their immense manpower and talents to give us these wonders.

Amazing structures are more than the Ancient Pyramids, an Eiffel Tower or a Sydney Opera House.

While we love all the buildings mentioned in this book, we have two personal favourites.

The futuristic design (known as Googie) of the 1950s and 60s saw the world go crazy for all things space age and out of this world. The Theme Building at the Los Angeles International airport, built in 1961, is a prime example of Googie architecture. A year later, when the cartoon classic, *The Jetsons* hit our screens, it was easy to see the futuristic Theme Building had heavily influenced and inspired the architecture of the Jetson family's world. And it was fun!

Our other favourite structure also belongs to the future – so much so it's not even built yet! Dubai's Dynamic Tower will see each of its 80 floors rotate individually, activated by voice commands. Because the floors all move separately, it means this truly dynamic Tower will never look the same twice. It will be a constantly changing piece of modern sculpture. More than just an amazing structure, it will be a work of art. The Dynamic Tower is expected to open in 2020.

We hope this book inspires you to go out and explore the world's most amazing structures, and maybe to design your very own.

Glen Williams, 2018.

The Pyramids of Ancient Egypt

Want to know how to walk like an Egyptian? Just build a pyramid. It's backbreaking work. You'll never walk the same way again!

They are structures of wonder and mystery. The pyramids of Giza never cease to capture our imaginations and their construction will forever remain a talking point.

For approximately 1,000 years, the Egyptian pharaohs chose to pass on to eternity by being buried in pyramids. Desert storms covered many of the pyramids up.

But excavators and adventurers and intrepid archaeologists through the years have managed to uncover these great wonders, obscured by the winds of time and the smothering desert sands.

There are said to be about 90 pyramids known today. The best preserved and indeed the most famous are the ones at Giza, not far from Egypt's capital, Cairo.

The pyramids of Giza were the first of the Seven Wonders of the World. These pyramids were built approximately 4,500 years ago during the reigns of the Pharaohs Khufu, Khafre and Menkaure.

It took 20 years to build the largest pyramid, which was the burial place for Pharaoh Khufu. More than two million huge blocks of limestone were used in the making of this incredible structure. When it was completed it stood at 146 meters high. The ancient Egyptians can lay claim to building the first true skyscraper.

So How Were The Pyramids Built?

Opinions vary as to how the Great Pyramids of Giza were built. There were no cranes to hurl the massive blocks into place; no trucks, forklifts or conveyer belts to get the materials needed to the construction zone.

Instead, it was brute force and clever planning that allowed the pyramids to take shape.

The massive limestone blocks, weighing about two tonnes each, were delivered to the building site on barges that came sailing down the River Nile. A system of canals allowed the barges to come directly to the building site at Giza.

Then came the backbreaking work of getting the stones into place. It is believed gangs of men using ropes and wooden rollers dragged the stones up slopes made from mud brick before they could then fix each block into its rightful place in the pyramid.

A new study carried out by physicists at the University of Amsterdam shows the clever Egyptians may have been able to move the massive stone blocks across the desert by wetting the sand in front of a sled-like contraption that was used to haul the incredibly heavy blocks.

The study showed that dampening the sand in front of the giant sled made the surface firmer and reduced the friction of the sled, allowing for smoother and easier movement.

The scientists came to this conclusion using clues gleaned from the ancient tombs. A wall painting discovered in the tomb of Djehutihotep, dating back approximately 1900 BC, shows 172 men hauling a gigantic statue using ropes attached to a sled. The drawing shows a person standing on the front of the sled, pouring water over the sand.

The team of scientists at the University of Amsterdam recreated this exercize by constructing miniature sleds and pulling heavy objects through trays of sand. When the researchers dragged their sleds across dry sand, the sand would build up in front of the sled and more manpower was needed to pull the sleds across.

When water was applied the sleds were able to glide more easily across the surface. The drops of water create bridges between the grains of sand allowing them to stick together. The scientists said this is also the reason it is better to use wet sand rather than dry when trying to build a sandcastle.

The team were quick to point out there is a very delicate balance when it comes to how damp the sand needs to be. They concluded that using dry sand makes the job of moving heavy objects harder, and also requires more manpower. But if the sand is too wet, it will be even more difficult.

Judging by the magnificent pyramids standing proudly before us, the Ancient Egyptians got the balance between dry and wet just right. It is believed their secret formula for moving success was 2 per cent water to 5 per cent of the volume of sand.

Clever people, and masterful engineers, those Ancient Egyptians.

(Source: Live Science. *www.livescience.com*, Uncovering The Past, Ancient Egypt.)

>> DID YOU KNOW? <<

- The Ancient Egyptian Pyramids of Giza are the most famous of pyramid structures.

- The Ancient Egyptian pyramids were mostly constructed as tombs for pharaohs and their families.

- The first pyramids had stepped sides so the king's soul could climb the stairs to reach heaven and the afterlife. The pyramids built later had smooth sloping sides. The sloping sides of the pyramids are believed to represent the sun's rays. It was believed the pharaoh's soul could climb up the rays to reach the sun god and the glorious, eternal afterlife.

- Over 130 pyramids have been discovered in Egypt.

- The Great Pyramid of Giza is the oldest and largest of the three pyramids in the Giza Necropolis. At the time of construction, the Great Pyramid stood at 280 Egyptian cubits tall (146.5 meters, or 480.6 feet). Sadly, with erosion and the loss of its pyramidion (the uppermost piece of a pyramid) the Great Pyramid now stands at 138.8 meters (455.4 feet). Each side of its base was 440 cubits (230.4 meters, or 755.9 feet) long. A true giant of the desert.

- The Great Pyramid is also known as the Pyramid of Khufu. It is the oldest of the Ancient Wonders of the World and the last one still largely intact.

- For over 3,800 years the Great Pyramid of Giza was the tallest man-made structure in the world.

- Nearly all Egyptian pyramids are found on the west bank of the Nile.

- The Egyptian pyramids contain a labyrinth of passageways and multiple chambers.

- Bodies placed in the tombs were preserved by mummification.

- Egyptians buried their dead with a host of burial goods, ranging from everyday items they believed would come in handy in the afterlife, to riches such as expensive jewellery, gold death masks and gilded thrones.

- The royal tombs, filled with the wealth of the pharaohs, became the targets of tomb robbers.

- One tomb left largely intact, and possibly the most famous, was that of Tutankhamun in the Valley of the Kings. That tomb was rediscovered in 1922 by Howard Carter. The tomb is best known for the solid gold funeral mask of Tutankhamun.

(Source: Science Kids www.sciencekids.co.nz , Great Civilizations Ancient Egypt, Discover Ancient Civilizations Ancient Egypt)

The solid gold funeral mask of Tutankhamun.

The Parthenon
– Athens, Greece

We have all heard the word 'acropolis'. It is a Greek word and means a high hill or 'upper city'. These upper cities were most important – this was where people would take shelter in times of trouble. From the upper city, the inhabitants could keep watch and prepare for any potential invasions.

The acropolis is also where many temples were built.

Wander up the hill that climbs heavenward behind Athens, and you will find the world's most famous acropolis. So famous, it's simply called 'The Acropolis. It sits above Athens, some 100 meters above the bustling Greek capital, its flat top housing a cluster of ancient temples.

When the sun shines, these spectacular temples glow whiter than white, like some ethereal cloud for the gods and godesses of Ancient Greece to drift upon and keep a vigilant watch.

The most breathtaking of these ancient temples nestled atop the Acropolis is The Parthenon.

Designed by the famous sculptor, Phidias, work on the stunning temple began in 447 BC. The Parthenon was built to honor Athens' patron goddess, Athena. Athena was the goddess of wisdom, warfare and courage.

More than just a building, more than a temple, the Parthenon stands as a symbol of the 'Golden Age Of Athens', where democracy was born. It also remains one of the world's most important pieces of architecture. While it did not present any engineering breakthroughs in building construction, its design became the benchmark for buildings all around the world – and still is today. Just go to any town and city around the world and you will find countless buildings influenced by – and looking like poor relations of – the Parthenon.

Standing 13.716 meters (45 feet) tall, and with a base 69.49 meters (228 feet) by 30.78 meters (101 feet), the Parthenon's enormous foundations are made of limestone. Its trademark columns are made of Pentelic marble, a material used for the first time in this building.

While it was designed by Phidias, construction of the Parthenon (which continued until 438 BC) was supervized by architects Callicrates and Ictinos. Decoration of the temple continued for another six years after construction was completed.

In her 2,500 plus year life, the Parthenon has had some tough times. She has been shaken by earthquakes, set on fire, shattered by exploding gun powder, looted and plundered of her treasures, and sadly defaced during what has been described as 'misguided preservation efforts'. And yet, on the whole, she is still standing.

Statue of Athena, patron goddess of Athens.

Elgin Marbles. Part of a Parthenon frieze now found in the British Museum.

Greece Wants Its Plundered Parthenon Treasures Returned

Many of the amazing treasures and art of the Parthenon cannot in fact be found in the Parthenon, but in the British Museum, London.

A British diplomat and art collector, Lord Thomas Elgin was sent to Athens to gather up works of art and to prevent France from dominating this greedy trade. In July 1801 Elgin ordered the last remaining statues of the Parthenon be seized. He also took pieces from other temples across the Acropolis. Famously, he took 55 marble slabs from a frieze in the Parthenon. These are now known as the 'Elgin Marbles', and they hold pride of place in the British Museum. People around the world were outraged by these so-called 'acquisitions'. The famous poet Lord Byron considered it no better than vandalism. Elgin argued that he had permission from the Turkish government, who were occupying Greece at the time. Elgin himself made a lot of money. He didn't donate: he sold the marbles to the British Museum. There are many Greeks, indeed many from all around the world who want this 'theft' righted and the works returned to Greece. The Greek Government has been fighting for them to be returned since the 1980s. The British Government, thus far, has refused to return the works.

Q: What is Pentelic marble?

A: This marble was mined from the quarries of Penteli, north of Athens. Mount Pentelicus has become famous for its marble, which was used first in the construction of the Parthenon then on other buildings atop the Acropolis and across Ancient Athens. Pentelic marble is a flawless white with a faint yellow tint which makes it shine with a golden hue under sunlight.

>> MORE FASCINATING FACTS ABOUT THE PARTHENON <<

- The Parthenon is an example of Doric style architecture, which is a simple style with plainer columns than other styles.

- The roof and the interior of the sanctuary were destroyed in the 3rd century AD by fire. In the 4th century AD the roof was replaced. The new roof was made of wood taken from the defeated Persian boats following the Greek naval victory at Salamis.

- In 435 AD, after 1,000 years as a temple dedicated to Greek goddess Athena, the Byzantine Emperor Theodosius II closed all the pagan temples. This saw the Parthenon and other temples of the Acropolis being looted and defaced.

- In the late 6th century AD the Parthenon was converted to a Christian church.

- In 1456 the Turkish Ottoman Empire invaded and by the end of the century the Parthenon was converted to a mosque.

- In 1687 when the Venetians attacked Athens, the Parthenon was severely damaged. The Ottomans had been storing ammunition inside the temple and it suffered an explosion when a mortar hit.

- The 1687 explosion destroyed the Parthenon's roof, blew out the central portion of the building, destroyed many columns on all sides, and killed approximately 300 people.

- Greece gained control of Athens in 1832, and all evidence of the Ottomans on the Acropolis was destroyed.

- The first known photograph of the Parthenon was taken in October,1839. The mosque in the Parthenon was still present at the time the photograph was taken.

- Some of the sculptures from the Parthenon are on display at the Louvre in Paris, France, and in Copenhagen, Denmark. The majority of the statues can be found in Athens' Acropolis Museum.

- Some efforts to preserve the Parthenon in the 1900s resulted in further damage. Marble cracked when rust from uncoated stabilizing pins expanded.

The Colosseum
– Rome, Italy

It looms just east of the Roman Forum. Many claim they can hear the screams of falling gladiators and terrified Christians being fed to the lions echoing from its ancient ruins.

Built rather hurriedly beginning 72 AD and completed ahead of schedule in 80 AD, the Colosseum was the most spectacular amphitheater of its time and the largest amphitheater ever built.

Construction on the Colosseum began under Emperor Vespasian and was completed and opened by his successor, Titus.

Built of travertine, tuff, brick, concrete and marble, it is believed these sturdy materials have allowed the Colosseum to stand the tests of time. It took approximately 30,000 slaves as well as many engineers and skilled workers to bring the spectacular project together.

The Colosseum stood grandly in the heart of Ancient Rome at 49 meters high, 188 meters long and 156 meters wide. The central arena is an oval shape and measures 87 meters (287 feet) long and 55 meters (180 feet) wide.

The Colosseum could hold between 50,000 and 80,000 spectators. The average audience was said to be about 65,000.

Unlike earlier Greek theaters that were built into hillsides, the Colosseum is entirely a freestanding structure.

Modern arenas still use the basic plan of the Colosseum which involved filling the arena quickly and evacuating it even more quickly. This was done by having the arena ringed by 80 entrances at ground level, 76 of which were used by ordinary spectators. Each entrance and exit was numbered as they are in the modern arenas of today. The northern main entrance was reserved for the Roman emperor and his aides, and the other three were reserved for Rome's elite. Their seats were made of fine polished marble. The lowest floor had the best view of the entertainment while the upper levels were held for the lower social classes and women.

Don't vomit! It's only an exit that allows you to leave in a hurry

Spectators were given tickets made of pottery upon which was inscribed what section they were in and their seat number, much like today – only our tickets are paper or computer-generated E-Tickets.

They accessed their seats via what was called a 'vomitorium', or (the plural) 'vomitoria'. These were passageways that opened into a tier of seats from below or behind – just like theaters of today. The vomitoria quickly dispersed people to their seats and, upon conclusion of the event or in the case of an emergency evacuation, could allow for their quick exit within only a few minutes.

Interestingly, the name 'vomitoria' comes from the Latin word meaning 'rapid discharge', from which the English language gets the word 'vomit'. So in case of an emergency, spectators at the Colosseum were literally spewing out of the vomitoria!

Blood and gore left them in awe

The Ancient Romans loved blood sports. The crowds came in droves to be titillated and entertained with an assortment of gore and horror.

Gladiators displayed their bravery by fighting to the death. Exotic animals including rhinoceroses, elephants, giraffes, lions, panthers, leopards and bears, hippopotamuses, crocodiles and ostriches would be mercilessly and cruelly hunted before being killed.

The crowds bayed for blood and loved it even more when a Christian or some other criminal condemned to die would be led into the arena naked and unarmed to face the wild beasts that awaited them. Lions were used mostly in this game of 'Get the Christians'. The victim could only run for so long before the hungry beast would catch them and literally tear the victim to shreds.

Entertainment also included acrobats and magicians, but the Romans mainly wanted their shows to involve torture, horror, blood, guts and gore – and ultimately a merciless death.

The Colosseum stopped being used for entertainment during the Middle Ages. It fell into disrepair, the southern side was destroyed in an earthquake and some of the materials were salvaged and used in the construction of other iconic Roman buildings, including St Peter's Basilica.

Today, the Colosseum is one of Rome's most popular tourist attractions. While the building underwent a major restoration between 1993 and 2000, it can now only seat a few hundred spectators in temporary seating. But that hasn't stopped the shows going on!

The Colosseum has been a backdrop for huge concerts staged by performers including Ray Charles, Billy Joel, Elton John and Paul McCartney.

A structure people find hard to stop staring at, the Colosseum will always be the true star. She is still the grand lady of Rome.

>> DID YOU KNOW? <<

- To celebrate the opening of the Colosseum, the emperor staged a 100-day festival of games. These games included much blood and gore, with gladiator fights to the death and animal spectacles. No one knows how many humans lost their lives during the festival but more than 9,000 animals were killed cruelly in the name of entertainment during those 100 days.

- There were thousands of caged wild animals kept beneath the Colosseum. These cages could be raised up through the many trap doors to suddenly appear in the middle of the arena. The cries of the agitated and terrified animals would have been drowned out by cheers and leers from the audience.

- The arena itself had a sand floor to absorb the blood that ran freely on a regular basis.

- The Colosseum was originally called Ampitheatrum Flavium.

- The Colosseum was ahead of its time with an enormous canvas awning that protected spectators from the hot Italian sun. It took approximately 1,000 men to put up the awning.

- It is thought that over 500,000 people lost their lives and over a million wild animals were killed during the Colosseum's people vs. beast games.

- The Ancient Romans would sometimes flood the Colosseum and have miniature naval ship battles.

- The Colosseum only took ten years to build, using the labor of over 60,000 Jewish slaves.

- The Colosseum has been subject to many natural disasters. It was the earthquakes of 847 AD and 1231 AD that caused most of the damage we see today.

- All Ancient Romans had free entry to the Colosseum for events. They were also generously fed throughout the spectacles while the not-so-lucky Christians were fed to the lions!

- The animal fighting spectacles staged at the Colosseum saw whole species of animals killed off. The number of lions, tigers and jaguars plummeted across the globe. Roman hunting of these animals saw the wildlife of North Africa devastated. Creatures like the hippo disappeared from the Nile and the North African elephant was completely wiped off the face the earth.

- The Colosseum is the world's 39th most popular tourist destination, with around four million tourists a year.

Source: Eyewitness Guides Ancient Rome, Ancient and Medieval People The Roman Gladiators, Wikipedia, Around Rome Tours

Stonehenge
– Wiltshire, United Kingdom

The great Stone Age circle of mystery never ceases to enthral.

What is a henge?
A prehistoric monument consisting of a circle of stone or wooden uprights. —Oxford Dictionary

It must have been eerie...some five thousand years ago, on a mist-shrouded Wiltshire field, a group of Stone Age people stopped to marvel at giant stones, standing tall, rising up from the marshy earth.

The giant oblong sarsen rocks reach a height of 4.572 meters (15 feet).

This site, known as Stonehenge was of great importance to the Stone Age community of the Salisbury Plains. It would weather the test of time and become possibly the world's most famous prehistoric monument.

Foreboding and creepy, this monumental structure was built in several stages. The first was a somewhat primitive example of an early henge (see above for definition of henge), built approximately 5,000 years ago. The unique and mysterious stone circle that we have all come to know was erected about 2500 BC, during what is known as the Neolithic Period. In the early Bronze Age it became a place of cremation and burial making Stonehenge the largest cemetery in the British Isles at the time.

Stonehenge has long been shrouded in mystery and speculation. It has been claimed the site was built as a pagan temple. Others claim it was an evil place where animal sacrifice and – even more grisly – *human* sacrifice was carried out; this is due to the discovery of a slab in the innermost circle that became known as the Slaughter Stone.

In the Middle Ages, many claimed the monument was linked to Merlin, the Welsh magician who performed magic for the legendary King Arthur. Others said it was a place of reverential worship for the Druids,

What is a Solstice?
Two occasions during the year when the sun is at its greatest distance from the celestial equator. This happens on June 21 and December 22. The Summer Solstice in the Northern Hemisphere (June 21) is the longest day of the year. The Winter Solstice (December 22) is the shortest day of the year. In the Southern Hemisphere it's the opposite: the longest day (Summer) is December 22 and the shortest day (Winter) is June 21.

population. There was a theory that Stonehenge was a temp devoted to worshiping the sun. To this day people of varying backgrounds and religions pilgrimage there to herald the arrival of the English summer – or Summer Solstice – on June 21. They also come to celebrate the Winter Solstice in December.

Many archaeologists think Stonehenge was built as a temple for the observation of the stars and astronomical phenomena They believe the great stones placed in a circle were some so of calendar that showed farmers (agriculture was the main industry at the time) the various starts of each season.

More recent claims see Stonehenge as a healing center, where pilgrims came to be cured from sickness and injury.

Basically there are many theories about this incredible monument located 130 kilometers (80 miles) west of Londo However, it remains unclear today exactly why Stoneheng was built. And that's part of the magic of the place.

How did the stones of Stonehenge stand up by themselves?

And how on earth did they get the Lintels to lie on top of them?

During the periods in which it was constructed (it stretched out over 1,500 years) there were no cranes and no forklifts.

How on earth, then, did they manage to get the giant stones – weighing a whopping 27 tons (25 metric tonnes) – to stand up, and how did they place the Lintel stones on top?

According to the book *Enigmas Of History, The Mysteries of Stonehenge*, 'Stonehenge represents a colossal effort of planning and execution. The monument took on diverse forms over 40 generations of existence.'

Moving The Stones: The stones were brought from a great distance on foot. Many of the stones were brought to the site being rolled over logs, which acted like a Stone Age conveyer belt. It is believed the stones came from Wales and were transported by rafts along the River Avon.

Positioning: At the site, a circular pit was dug and the stones were pushed into the pit using levers and tree trunks.

The Menhirs: The giant rocks standing upright are called Menhirs. Once the Menhirs were in the pit they were hoisted upright using ropes, with approximately 150 men pulling tug-of-war style to position them. The Menhirs were buried somewhat deep to set them into the ground.

Placement of Lintels: The rocks lying across the top of the Menhirs are known as Lintels. It is believed the Lintels were raised using a tower of tree trunks that was erected in a crisscrossing manner. Again manpower was used along with that clever invention the wooden lever to lift the Lintel and allow another layer of tree trunks to be placed beneath it. As the tower grew in height, the lintel would finally be atop the Menhirs and moved into place.

>> DID YOU KNOW THIS ABOUT STONEHENGE? <<

- Stonehenge was constructed over three phases spanning centuries (approximately 1,500 years). It is estimated the construction required more than thirty million hours of labor.

- It remains a mystery as to why it was built. Speculation is varied, ranging from a temple for human sacrifice to a laboratory for astronomy.

- There is a long avenue connecting the monument to the River Avon. This is simply called The Avenue.

- Two types of stone make up Stonehenge; the larger known as sarsen stones and the smaller known as bluestones.

- The largest of the rocks stands at 4.572 meters (15 feet, or roughly the size of three men standing on each other's shoulders).

- The largest rocks weigh approximately 27 tons, or 25 metric tonnes.

- It is estimated that it took approximately 150 men to raise the rocks and set them in place.

- The outer ring of Stonehenge is made up of vertical, oblong-shaped sandstone. Inside the outer circle is another circle made up of the smaller bluestone.

- It is believed the bluestones came from the Pressell Mountains in South Wales, which are said to have healing qualities. Hence it is widely believed Stonehenge was built as a Stone Age healing center and health retreat.

- On June 21 and December 22 each year, thousands of pilgrims from all around the world flock to Stonehenge to celebrate the Summer and Winter Solstice.

- Some people believe that aliens built Stonehenge but there has not been any proof of this theory. Stonehenge is often referred to when people discuss crop circles.

- Stonehenge holds great religious significance for neo-Druidry. In 1905 there was a mass initiation of Druids held by the Ancient Order of Druids at Stonehenge. They were said to have worn white robes and fake beards during the initiation. Any ritual use is now restricted. As a result, Druids have erected Stonehenge-type monuments in other places around the world.

- In 2008 archaeological evidence was uncovered that suggests Stonehenge may have been a burial site even before Stonehenge itself was built.

- Those who built Stonehenge had to have been extremely sophisticated in mathematics and geometry.

- Stonehenge features in several motion pictures including: *This Is Spinal Tap* (1984), *The Black Knight* (1954), *King Lear* (1971), *King Arthur* (2004), *National Lampoon's European Vacation* (1985), *The Misfits of Avalon* (2001) *Merlin of the Crystal Cave* (1991) and *Merlin: The Return* (2000).

- Stonehenge is considered to be a masterpiece in engineering.

The Great Wall Of China

It isn't called the Great Wall of China for nothing! And it's little wonder it is considered one of the Wonders of the World!

Originally built to keep foreign invaders out, the Great Wall of China now plays host to millions of foreign tourists each year.

The Wall has the honor of being the longest structure ever built. The length depends on who is measuring it and whether they consider every section of the Great Wall, including the parts that deviate away from the main wall. Overall the Wall stretches for a whopping 22,000 kilometers (13,670 miles). The length of the main wall is approximately 6,300 kilometers (3,915 miles).

Why the need to build such a huge Wall?

China flourished on the fertile plains of East Asia. They thrived with a number of healthy rivers, and they made great advances in developing farming technology. But China's neighbors toiled on barren lands for little reward, so they looked with jealousy and envy upon the successful China.

Although China was protected by the looming Himalayas, the inhospitable Tibetan Plateau, and the broad Pacific Ocean to the east, she lay open to attack in the north and northwest of her empire. The Mongol, Turkish and Xiongnu tribes were just waiting to invade.

China's flat terrain also made it easier for looters and invaders to carry out their invasions.

The solution? A great, big, gigantic, monstrous wall. Well, to start with it was a series of several different walls all being blended together. The Great Wall was not constructed under one single emperor but several. Different parts were constructed over different centuries. In fact it was the ultimate ongoing DIY project that the Chinese just couldn't get enough of. It took a staggering

2,000 years before they were finally happy with their fancy garden wall. The wall was built and rebuilt when erosion came calling, it was extended and heightened...and so it went on. The Ming Dynasty (1368–1644) were the last group to renovate. It was only then that the Wall went from being pretty impressive to truly Great!

Who Helped To Build The Great Wall?

Chinese soldiers were the first to start construction on the wall. Emperor Qin Shihuang ordered around 300,000 soldiers to defend the site and to build the Wall after they defeated the invading Huns.

Besides soldiers, the Emperor also forced common people to join the mammoth construction project. Other dynasties would also adhere to the Emperor's brutal actions and more and more common folk were forced into virtual slavery to construct the Great Wall. There is a portion of wall stretching more than 450 kilometers (280 miles) between Xiakou and Hengzhou that was built solely by common people.

The Sui Dynasty (581–618 AD), was even harsher, forcing widows to take up building the Wall as the supply of male laborers had run out.

Convicted criminals were to build the Wall as part of their punishment. The criminals could be identified by their shaved heads and by the clanging of iron rings and chains around their ankles. They were forced to work on the Wall at night and were required to labor for four years, according to the laws of the Qin Dynasty.

There is no accurate record showing how many people helped build the Great Wall of China, but given that construction took approximately 2,500 years it is estimated conservatively that around 3,700,000 people were forced to work – and many to die – upon that gigantic wall.

Dead Bodies Are Part Of The Wall.

It is strongly believed the Great Wall of China is riddled with the dead bodies of the millions of workers who perished during its construction. Due to the pressing schedule to complete the mammoth project, authorities deemed it too much of a waste of time to cart away the constant stream of dead bodies for a decent burial. This led to a much spoken-of belief that the Great Wall of China is haunted by the many troubled souls who were worked to death upon its rambling ramparts.

>> GREAT WALL ENGINEERING FACTS
WE BET YOU DIDN'T KNOW! <<

- Construction material for the Great Wall of China consisted mainly of earth, wood, stones, sand and bricks, depending on era of construction. When building over mountain ranges, the stones of the mountain were used. These included granite, marble, limestone, and shale – all used to make just another brick in the Wall!

- The Great Wall's main purpose was to guard against invasions and attacks from the north.

- The Great Wall of China is the longest structure ever built by humans.

- The widest section of the Wall is around 9 meters (30 feet).

- The highest point of the Wall is around 8 meters (26 feet).

- The first parts of the Wall were built over 2,000 years ago.

- There was a huge loss of human life during the construction, estimated to be close to a million.

- Major rebuilding of the Great Wall of China took place during the Ming Dynasty, which began in the 14th century. Construction during this period was particularly strong due to the use of stone and brick. Prior to this the building materials were mainly stone, wood and compacted earth.

- Some of the well-maintained sections of the Wall, particularly those near Beijing, are particularly popular tourist destinations.

- While some parts of the Wall have been preserved or renovated, other parts have been vandalized or destroyed.

- It is widely believed that the Great Wall of China is so vast and far-reaching that astronauts can see it clearly with the naked eye from the moon. Sadly this notion has been debunked.

(Source: Science Kids Website. Fun Great Wall of China Facts for Kids. Wikipedia, *www.scienceabc, www.travelchinaguide. com_great_wall/facts/who-built.htm*

THE LEANING TOWER OF PISA

The Leaning Tower of Pisa
– Pisa, Italy

The tourists come in their thousands to the Piazza del Duomo in the Italian city of Pisa to gaze upon and photograph a humble belltower.

Mind you, this quirky building is now much more than a belltower; it has become one of the most talked about structures in the world.

The historical Leaning Tower Of Pisa is the home of the ultimate modern day fad, the selfie! Time and time again you can see people posing for the exact same photo. They stand with their hands outstretched towards the leaning belltower, as if they are stopping it from toppling over completely with their sheer might and strength.

Located next to the stunning Cathedral of Pisa in the aptly named Square of Miracles (Piazza del Miracoli), construction on the world's most famous belltower began in August 1173. By the time the Tower's builders made it to the third story, in 1178, the soft, marshy, shifting soil upon which it was built destabilized the Tower's foundations. It began to take on its renowned lean.

Construction was interrupted several times by wars, debt, and worried engineers at a loss to halt the Tower's leaning position. It was thanks to these lengthy interruptions that the soil beneath the Tower was allowed to compress. Had this not happened, the Tower would probably be called the Falling Tower of Pisa!

This settling stage lasted for over a century, before construction resumed in 1275. The Tower wasn't completed until the 14th century, in 1399.

For the following eight centuries, the 55-meter Tower wasn't just leaning but was actually *falling* at a rate of one to two millimeters per year. Italian officials say one day the Tower will topple. The lean will suddenly give way to a complete, tumbling, heavy fall. It's just a matter of time.

» FACTS ABOUT THE TOWER YOU PROBABLY DIDN'T KNOW! «

- Pisa was named in 600 BC. The name comes from a Greek word meaning 'marshy land'.

- There are other towers in Pisa that also lean. You can see a tilt on the tower at the church of Saint Michele degli Scalzi, and a definite hunch on the belltower at the church of Saint Nicola. Those two towers are said to be jealous that the Leaning Tower of Pisa gets all the fame and glory. It's like the Mona Lisa's sister, no one ever talks about her wayward smirk!

- While all eyes are focused on the Leaning Tower, the cathedral and baptistery next to it are also sinking.

- Galileo was baptized in the cathedral's baptistery in 1565.

- The Leaning Tower is built upon soft ground consisting of clay, fine sand and shells.

- The Leaning Tower is medieval architecture built in a Romanesque style.

- The Tower was built with limestone and lime mortar. The exterior is covered in marble. It is understood the limestone is the reason why the tower has not cracked and broken, because it is flexible enough to withstand the pressures placed on the structure by the dramatic lean.

- Even Mussolini had a go at trying to stabilize the Leaning Tower. He felt the Tower was an embarrassment to himself and to all of Italy, and that it must be put right and stand straight and tall. The dictator's orders were followed: 361 holes were drilled into the foundation and 90 tonnes of cement were poured to fill them. Unfortunately, the cement did not fill up the holes and act as the much needed counterweight, but rather sank into the clay beneath the building, causing the Tower to lean over even more. Mussolini was said to be furious and baying for blood.

- They closed the Tower again in 1990 for further construction and to ensure the Tower was safe for the ever-increasing onslaught of tourists. After several months the all clear was giving and it was open for business once again. All in all, it has taken over 800 years for the tower of Pisa to be finally constructed. This makes it not only a wonder to behold, but also the holder of the record for the longest construction time in the world.

How Tall, How Wide And How Many Steps Inside?

- The completed height of the Leaning Tower of Pisa was 60 meters. In reality the Tower's official height is 56.67 meters on the highest side and 55.86 meters on the lowest side.

- The outside diameter at the base is 15.484 meters.

- The width of the walls at the base is 2.4384 meters.

- The Tower weighs approximately 14,500 tonnes.

- There are 251 steps from the bottom to the top of the Pisa Tower.

The Taj Mahal
– Agra, India

A Building Devoted To The Wonders of Love.

The moment it comes into view – all white and shimmering, dreamlike, almost a mirage – this most famous of buildings leaves you breathless.

But this is no mirage, it's simply known as the Taj!

It was commissioned to be built in 1632 by the grieving, love-struck Mughal emperor Shah Jahan to house the remains of his wife, Arjumand Banu Begum, who was lovingly called Mumtaz Mahal – 'Chosen One of the Palace'.

Indeed she was the chosen one; she was said to be the most cherished and beloved of his three queens.

In 1631, after giving birth to their fourteenth child, Mumtaz Mahal sadly died. The grieving Emperor was inconsolable. He ordered the building of a grand mausoleum, a structure like no other ever seen in the world. He wanted this grand design built across the Yamuna River so he could gaze upon it at all times from his royal palace at Agra.

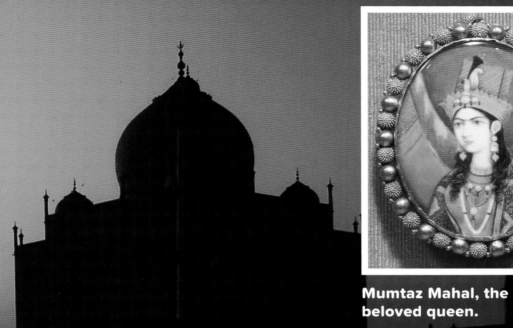

Mumtaz Mahal, the beloved queen.

>> DID YOU KNOW? <<

- Construction began in approximately 1632 and would take 20 years to complete.

- The chief architect was Ustad Ahmad Lahouri, an Indian of Persian descent. He would go on to also design the magnificent Red Fort in New Delhi. The Red Fort and the Taj Mahal are two of the most visited sites in India.

- More than 20,000 workers from Persia, India, Europe and the Ottoman Empire toiled long and hard on the construction of this opulent mausoleum devoted to endless love.

- Along with man power, 1,000 elephants were brought in to handle the heavy lifting.

- The Taj Mahal was made of white marble that mysteriously changes color depending on the direction of the sunlight and moonlight hitting its gleaming surface.

- The marble is inlaid with semi-precious stones: jade, lapis lazuli, crystal, amethyst and turquoise.

- The central dome reaches a height of 73 meters. The main dome is surrounded by four smaller domes. Four minarets stand at each corner of the complex.

- In keeping with Islamic tradition, verses from the Qur'an are inscribed on the arched entrances to the mausoleum.

- Once inside there is an octagonal marble chamber adorned with carvings and more semi-precious stones. This is known as the 'false tomb'. The real tomb, housing the sarcophagus containing the remains of the beloved queen, lies directly below at the same level as the garden.

- It is believed, but not confirmed, that Shah Jahan had his servants cut off the hands of the Taj Mahal's architect and his workers after the building was completed so they could never build another of its kind.

Plans for a Twin Taj Mahal

Legend has it that, despite the Emperor not wanting another structure like the masterpiece that is the Taj Mahal, he had intended building a matching second mausoleum directly across the river. They would sit like complimentary bookends.

The two structures were to be connected by a bridge. It was the Emperor's vision that his spirit would meet that of his wife on the bridge, their love would be inflamed and they would be together for eternity.

Sadly this was not to be as the ailing Emperor was deposed by his own son, Aurangzeb, who was his third oldest boy. Aurangzeb seized power in 1658 and had his father put under house arrest.

The loving Emperor Shah Jahan lived out his final years locked up in a tower in the Red Fort at Agra, where he could gaze, broken-hearted, upon the magnificent and majestic resting place he had constructed for his beloved wife. When he died in 1666 there was no matching mausoleum constructed for him – he was buried, rather fittingly, in the Taj Mahal, right next to his beautiful, much-loved queen.

The Most Inspirational Building In The World?

They come from all corners of the world. Pilgrims, sightseers, lovers of architecture, lovers of love; young and old come to gaze upon the opulent majesty of the Taj Mahal.

Some 45,000 people a day flock to Agra to glimpse this most revered of structures.

The poor, the struggling, the rich, the famous. Who could forget the sad shadow cast by a forlorn Princess Diana, who came to the Taj alone to seek comfort by the mausoleum's tranquil pools back on February 11, 1992. Diana sat pensively, reflecting on her troubled marriage. A few short years later her separation and ultimate divorce from Prince Charles would become final.

Then, as if to restore the Taj Mahal's image as a palace devoted to love, Diana's son Prince William, Duke of Cambridge, and his beautiful wife Catherine, Duchess of Cambridge, posed happily at the Taj in the very same place where Diana had cast such a sad and lonely figure.

But the elements of a highly industrialized modern India put the Taj constantly at risk. Air pollution from nearby factories sully the trademark gleaming white marble façade.

In 1988 the Supreme Court of India ordered a number of air-pollution measures to protect the building from the ever-present threat of irreversible deterioration. Many factories were forced to close, while India's frenzied and chaotic traffic has been banned completely from the area surrounding the famed structure.

For now the Taj Mahal remains one of the most inspirational and cherished structures in the world. For now she still evokes love and wonder, and she still gleams that magical white, shimmering in sunlight and glowing by the light of India's famously luminous full moons.

The Eiffel Tower
– Paris, France

In 2017 the Eiffel Tower, or the 'Iron Lady' as she is widely called, celebrated her 300 millionth visitor.

Without doubt this striking tower – which has loomed over Paris since opening on March 31 1889 – is one of the most famous structures in the world and easily one of the most popular tourist attractions.

The Eiffel Tower, or La Tour Eiffel as the French call her, was the 'wow factor' of the World's Fair staged in Paris in 1889.

It was built to commemorate a hundred years since the French Revolution and to show off France's industrial prowess to the world.

There had never been a structure like it, and the world marvelled. Wrought iron was the new big thing in building materials and thanks to the Industrial Revolution would become 'the thing' to use in modern architecture.

Famous architect, Gustave Eiffel.

Gustave Eiffel, a French civil engineer, is the man usually associated with giving the world the Eiffel Tower, but it was two lesser known engineers, Maurice Koechlin and Emile Mouguier, who came up the striking tower's original drawings. They worked for Eiffel's engineering firm, Compagnie des Etablissements Eiffel. Along with Eiffel and a French architect, Stephen Sauvestre, they submitted their plans to a contest that would decide the centerpiece for the 1889 World's Fair in Paris. And they won!

Construction of the wrought-iron tower began in July 1887.

Not everyone was thrilled with this gigantic iron monstrosity looming over Paris. Paris' Bohemian and artistic community howled with protests. They pleaded with Eiffel to halt construction of the 'ridiculous tower' that would dominate Paris like a 'gigantic black smokestack'.

But as they say, 'you can't stop progress'. The artists' grumblings fell on deaf ears. The Eiffel Tower soared to the heavens and was completed in just over two years, on March 31, 1889.

Construction of the Eiffel Tower.

There had never been a construction process like it. Every bit of the tower was planned down to the most minute detail.

Each of the 18,000 pieces used to build the tower was calculated specifically for this one project and prepared in Eiffel's huge factory on the outskirts of Paris.

The Eiffel Tower was made up of four huge arched legs, set on masonry piers that curved inward until they joined in a single tapered tower.

The structure required 2.5 million thermally assembled rivets and 7,300 tons of iron.

To protect the tower from the elements, every bit of the tower was painted. This staggering feat required 60 tonnes of paint. In its lifetime, the Eiffel Tower has been painted too many times to count.

Of the many of hundreds of construction workers involved in the building of the Eiffel Tower, there was only one fatality. A construction worker who was off duty at the time was showing his family around the site when he plunged to his death. Many give credit for the low death toll to the extensive use of guard rails and safety screens – a new phenomenon in construction at the time.

The Statue of Liberty's little sister, by the River Seine in Paris.

>> DID YOU KNOW THIS ABOUT THE EIFFEL TOWER? <<

- The Eiffel Tower is 320 meters (1,050 feet) in height and was the tallest man made structure in the world for 41 years, before the Chrysler Building in New York soared past it.

- The Eiffel Tower is made of iron and weighs around 10,000 tonnes.

- Millions of people climb the tower every year and it has had over 250 million visitors since its opening.

- Around 50 tonnes of paint are added to the Eiffel Tower every 7 years to protect it from rust.

- It is said that the Eiffel Tower, despite its height, is wind resistant. It sways only a few inches in the heaviest of winds. The tower actually moves further when the iron on the sun-facing side of the structure heats and expands.

- Temperature, believe it or not, also alters the height of the Eiffel Tower by up to six inches (15 centimeters).

- The Eiffel Tower has 108 storeys, with 1,710 steps. However, visitors can only climb stairs to the first platform. There are two elevators.

- The Eiffel Tower is so popular it has been recreated around the world including the half scale replica at the Paris Las Vegas Hotel in Nevada, USA, and the full scale Tokyo Tower in Japan.

- The Eiffel Tower took two years, two months and five days to complete.

- It cost 7,799,401.31 in French francs to build the Eiffel Tower. No one can quite work out what that would be today, but it's a lot.

- In 1944 after the Nazis had invaded and occupied France, Adolph Hitler ordered the German military governor of France to tear down the Eiffel Tower, but this order was bravely refused.

- Over the years the Eiffel Tower – like a Paris high fashion model – has kept abreast of style trends. When it opened in 1889, it wore a reddish-brown coat. A decade later it was painted a summery yellow. It later became yellow-brown, then chestnut brown, before the adoption of the current specially mixed 'Eiffel Tower Brown', in 1968.

- The Eiffel Tower was once the world's largest billboard. When dusk fell across Paris between 1925 and 1936, 250,000 colored light bulbs attached to three sides of the tower's steeple lit up to spell the 100-foot vertical letters of the French automobile company Citroen. So bright was the glaring advertisement it was visible from 20 miles away, and aviator Charles Lindbergh used it as a guiding beacon when he landed in Paris on his 1927 solo trans-Atlantic flight.

- Gustave Eiffel was hired to work on another world-famous landmark. During the construction of the Statue of Liberty, a gift of the French to the United States, the initial designer died suddenly in 1879. Gustave Eiffel was quickly hired to take his place. Eiffel designed the skeletal support system to which the statue's copper skin would be affixed. Today, a scale model of the Statue of Liberty stands on an island in the River Seine; in the shadow of the engineer's greatest work, the Eiffel Tower.

The Empire State Building
– New York, USA

The Birth Of The Modern Sky Scraper.

As long as humans have walked the planet, we have been reaching for the stars. Eyes always glancing heaven-ward, our primary interest has long been about making things, taller, grander, bigger, higher.

In Biblical times they tried it with the Tower of Babel – a foolish plan to build a way of getting to heaven before being called by God. That attempt at what was hoped to not only be a sky scraper but one leading to Heaven's Door...failed dismally.

The building of the Empire State Building was more of a race; a crazy dash to construct the world's tallest and largest skyscraper.

It was the 1920s. Hopes were high and despite a looming, gloomy Depression,

New York's economy was booming and construction of tall buildings was happening all over Manhattan at a cracking pace.

The race for the world's tallest building began over at 40 Wall Street with the frenzied creation of the Bank Of Manhattan Building. Nearby, the Chrysler Building was also surging towards the sky. An elaborate, gleaming, Art Deco wonder, this was the brainchild of automobile magnate Walter Chrysler, who called the building 'a monument to me'.

The competition between the two towers was so fierce they kept adding extra floors to their designs, leaving engineers and builders scratching their heads and bracing themselves to venture – mostly without the strict safety standards of today – to heights man had never been to before. The construction of the modern skyscraper was a wonder to behold, but many men lost their lives plunging to their deaths from great heights as they walked the precarious steel beams, like you see tightrope walkers do at the Circus. The only difference is they were much higher up than any tightrope walker, and they had no safety net beneath to catch them should they fall. And hundreds, sadly, did.

The race to be the tallest building had a late entry when in August 1929, General Motors executive John J. Raskob and the former New York Governor Al Smith unveiled their plan for the Empire State Building.

When an outraged Chrysler heard the Empire State Building would

be 1,000 feet tall (304.8 meters) he changed his plans for the last time and added a shiny, stainless steel spire to the top of his monument. This brought the Chrysler Building to a soaring 1,048 feet (319.4304 meters).

Raskob and Smith simply laughed, shrugged their shoulders and came back with an even more grandiose – and taller – design for their Empire State Building.

On May 1, 1931, when President Herbert Hoover turned on the lights by hitting a switch in the White House in Washington, the New York jewel lit up like a Christmas tree and audible gasps could be heard all around the world. The Empire State Building, a gleaming colossus and homage to engineering and construction, dominated the New York skyline. Soaring a staggering 1,250 feet (381 meters), this 102-story Art Deco modern wonder loomed over the surging streets of Midtown Manhatten. This wondrous giant was now the tallest building in the world, and would remain so for nearly 40 years until the completion of the tragically ill-fated World Trade Center's first tower, constructed in 1970.

Rival skyscraper, the Chrysler Building.

>> DID YOU KNOW? <<

- Despite the monumental size of the project, the Empire State Building was completed in record time. The design, planning and construction of the skyscraper only took 20 months from start to finish.

- The construction, involving as many as 3,400 men each day, only took 410 days to complete.

- The project builders were mostly immigrants from Europe, along with hundreds of Mohawk iron workers, many from the Kahnawake reserve near Montreal.

- The building went up (and up and up!) at a staggering four and half storeys per week.

- The Empire State Building is composed of 60,000 tons of steel, 200,000 cubic feet of Indiana limestone and granite, 10 million bricks, and 730 tons of aluminum and stainless steel.

- According to official accounts, five workers died during the construction.

- The building's owners were convinced that airship travel was going to be the modern way to fly. They decided to turn the 200-foot tower (60.96 meters) into a docking port for the eye-catching, highly flammable dirigibles. It was a crazy scheme, not to mention hair-raising. It called for the airship to manoeuvre alongside the building and tether itself to the tower. The terrified passengers would then have to fight a case of severe vertigo and exit via an open-air gangplank hundreds of meters off the ground.

People readily embraced the idea, but constant high winds buffeting the rooftop made it near-impossible for even the most skilled of pilots to negotiate. There was one successful landing in September 1932 when a small airship managed to tether itself to the building's spire for a few short minutes. Shortly after, in what was deemed a publicity stunt, a Goodyear blimp dropped off a bundle of newspapers as if to say this is how papers would be delivered from now on. The airship plan was abandoned a few weeks later.

- More than 250 movies have been shot in and around the Empire State Building. The most famous is the 1933 classic, *King Kong,* which climaxes with the giant ape scaling the colossal landmark and swatting at swarming and tormenting biplanes. *An Affair To Remember* (1957), *Sleepless in Seattle* (1993), and *Independence Day* (1996) are just a few of the many movies to be inspired by the wonder that is the Empire State Building.

A Plane Crash And A Hair-Raising Lift Plunge.

It was a foggy morning in July 28, 1945. Heavy-set, pea soup-thick fog snaked its way around the New York skyline, causing the skyscrapers to all but vanish.

A B-52 bomber was making its way back to the airport. The skilled pilot, Lieutenant Colonel William Franklin Smith, Jr. – a World War II veteran – had managed to skirt his way around the minefield of skyscrapers that is Midtown Manhattan. Sadly he couldn't escape crashing into the Empire State Building. His B-52 ploughed into the 78th and 79th floors, causing a massive explosion and a four alarm fire to break out. At the time it was the highest building fire in the world. Miraculously, the New York Fire Department managed to extinguish the blaze in just 40 minutes and the building was again open for business a speedy two days later.

The pilot, two crewmen and eleven people working inside the building were all killed as a result of the crash.

But miracles happened as well. When the plane crashed, several pieces of the engine sliced through the building and entered the elevator shaft. The cables of two elevator cars were shredded including one containing Betty Lou Oliver, a 19-year-old elevator operator. Her elevator plunged from the 75th floor, hurtling at breakneck speed to the subbasement. Incredibly, luck was on Betty-Lou's side. Thousands of meters of severed elevator cable had fallen before her and gathered mattress-like at the bottom of the shaft. The cable was able to cushion the impact of Betty-Lou's fall. It was thought the terrifying plunge to certain death was also slowed by a pocket of compressed air caused by the car's swift descent. Betty-Lou suffered severe trauma and injuries, including a broken neck and back. But she survived. She vowed from that day on she would always take the stairs.

The Fight To Stay The Tallest Skyscraper In The World.

It was the first building in the world to exceed 100 floors and, despite no longer being the tallest building in the world, it remains the definitive symbol of New York.

There were plans to add more floors on to restore it to the position of tallest building in the world, but many protested that it would change the iconic look of one of the most famous buildings in the world.

It may not be the tallest any more: that honor belongs to the 829.8 meter tall (2,722 ft) *Burj Khalifa* in Dubai (of the United Arab Emirates). The building gained the official title of tallest building in the world, and the tallest self-supported structure, at its opening on January 9, 2010. Still, the Empire State Building is definitely one of the most loved. In a 2007 survey, the America Institute of Architects declared the Empire State Building to be 'America's favorite building'. In 1994 the landmark building was rightfully declared one of the Seven Wonders of the Modern World. Not content with that, she has often been called the Eighth Wonder of the World. There is no argument: they don't build them like that anymore. The Empire State Building certainly is a wonder.

Sydney Opera House
– Sydney, Australia

'It stands by itself as one of the indisputable masterpieces of human creativity, not only in the 20th century but in the history of humankind.' – Expert evaluation report to the UNESCO World Heritage Committee, 2007.

It began in the rain and would weather many storms and controversies during its construction. The creation of Australia's most recognisable building – the iconic Sydney Opera House – had more intense drama than any of the thousands of operas and ballets staged there since its official opening by Queen Elizabeth II on October 20 1973.

The Opera House, lit up for the Vivid Sydney festival.

On March 2, 1959, an excited crowd gathered in the rain, huddled under umbrellas to watch the ceremony marking the start of construction of the Sydney Opera House. The crowd, standing sodden as the first sod of soil was turned, were promised they were going to see a breathtaking triumph, a building like no other.

Only in Australia would you find an important structure mostly paid for by the funds received from a lottery. It was called the Opera House Lottery and this nation of gamblers readily embraced it. It's how things get done Down Under. 'You need a new class-room or hospital? Let's have a chicken raffle.' 'You need a new opera house? Simple, let's have a lottery!'

Danish architect Jørn Utzon's stunning design for the Sydney Opera House had been selected from thousands of entries. He arrived in Australia a week before the heavens opened and the rains fell. He brought with him a bronze plaque commemorating the ceremony which NSW Premier Joseph Cahill, one of the staunchest supporters of the Sydney Opera House project, screwed into place. The moment the plaque was secured, jackhammering started, immediately drowning out the enthusiastic crowd.

From that March 1959 day on, Bennelong Point began to be transformed. The podium rose up from soft land interspersed with pockets of seawater that had to be pumped full of concrete foundations in order for the land to be able to bear the enormous weight of the structure. This concreting had not been budgeted for and sent the project into debt by £3.5 million (Australian pounds being the currency at the time).

A combination of ancient and modernist influences, and built upon what had been a sacred site for thousands of years to the indigenous Gadigal people, the elegance of the Sydney Opera House was more like a sculpture than a building. It wasn't long before the people of Sydney – and indeed the world – realized they were getting a true landmark for the twentieth century; a structure so unique, it would forever be synonymous with inspiration and imagination. Quite simply it was a work of art.

Frank Gehry, a Pritzker Prize judge, summed it up best when he awarded the Opera House's architect, Jørn Utzon, architecture's highest award in 2003: 'Jørn Utzon made a building well ahead of its time, far ahead of available technology... a building that changed the image of an entire country.'

>> INTERESTING FACTS HEAPS MORE DRAMATIC THAN ANY OPERA! <<

- The Sydney Opera House sits on Bennelong Point. The famous point is named after Woollarawarre Bennelong, a senior man of the Eora people at the time of the arrival of the British colonizers in Australia in 1788.

- The original cost estimate to build the Sydney Opera House was AU $7 million, but the cost blew out to AU $102 million. It was largely paid for by a State Lottery.

- 233 designs were submitted for the Opera House international design competition held in 1956. Jørn Utzon from Denmark was announced the winner, receiving £5,000 for his design.

- Construction was expected to take four years. It took fourteen!

- Work commenced in 1959 and involved 10,000 construction workers.

- The Sydney Opera House was added to UNESCO's World Heritage List in 2007.

- There are more than 1 million roof tiles (covering approximately 1.62 hectares) sitting over the structure. The tiles were made in Sweden.

- The Opera House uses 6,225 square meters of glass and 645 kilometers of electric cable.

- The Opera House roof sections are held together by 350 kilometres of tensioned steel cable.

- The Opera House has an annual audience of 2 million people for its performances.

- 200,000 people attend guided tours of the Opera House each year. More than 8.2 million people visit the landmark structure each year.

- Paul Robeson was the first person to perform at the Opera House. In 1960, he climbed the scaffolding and sang 'Ol' Man River' to the construction workers as they ate lunch.

- The Opera House is 185 meters long and 120 meters wide. Seven A380 jetliners could sit wing to wing on the site.

- Queen Elizabeth opened the Opera House on October 20, 1973. She has since visited four times, most recently in 2006.

- When the Sydney Symphony Orchestra is on stage in the Concert Hall, the temperature must be 22.5 degrees to ensure the instruments stay in tune. Temperature and humidity are critical to musical instruments.

- There are 1,000 rooms within the soaring sails of the Sydney Opera House.

- The Opera House stages 3,000 events each year.

- Arnold Schwarzenegger won his final Mr Olympia body building title in 1980 in the Concert Hall.

- A net was installed above the orchestra pit in the Joan Sutherland Theatre during the 1980s following an incident during the opera *Boris Godunov*. The opera featured live chickens and one walked off the stage, landing on top of a cellist.

- The Sydney Opera House is kept cool by using seawater taken directly from Sydney Harbour. The system circulates cold water through 35 kilometers of pipes to power both the heating and air conditioning in the building.

- Each year, Chinese New Year is celebrated at the Opera House by lighting its landmark sails in red. The sails are often used for special lighting effects to mark important national and international days.

- Many of the world's biggest showbiz names have clamored to perform at the Sydney Opera House. They include: Dame Joan Sutherland, Dame Kiri Te Kanawa, Luciano Pavarotti, Bob Hope, Olivia Newton-John, Helen Reddy, Nana Mouskouri, Ella Fitzgerald, Bangarra Dance Theatre, and folk group Peter, Paul and Mary. And who could forget both the Crowded House concerts in the Opera House Forecourt? They were two of the most-watched concerts in the world.

- Today the Sydney Opera House is known as one of the busiest performing arts centers in the world.

Source for these facts: Sydney Opera House website

Karakoram Highway
– China and Pakistan

As The Doors' song goes: 'Keep your eyes on the road and your hands upon the wheel.' Very appropriate advice for those brave enough to traverse the Karakoram Highway between Pakistan and China.

Breathtaking, astounding, and downright terrifying, the Karakoram Highway wends its way for 1,300 kilometers from China to Pakistan.

Also known as the Friendship Highway, work on this engineering marvel began in 1959 and officially opened to much fanfare in 1979.

The Highway is considered to be one of the most incredible engineering feats of the century; it is often referred to as the Eighth Wonder of the World. But such plaudits came at great cost, not only financially, but in the time it took to build and indeed the number of lives lost during its construction. Over 140 Chinese and approximately 810 Pakistani workers lost their lives while working on the mammoth project.

The Highway was promoted as a symbol of Pakistan-Chinese friendship and co-operation, and a boon for tourism in the perilous mountain region. It has also served as a road of strategic military importance.

During the fight over Kashmir between India and Pakistan, the Chinese and Pakistanis used the Highway to transport military equipment.

According to the March 1994 National Geographic, the silkworm missiles that China got in trouble for selling to Pakistan came via the Karakoram Highway. The Highway's bridges are said to be constructed to handle heavy military equipment and tanks.

Tourists, particularly lovers of the world's highest mountains, flock to use the highway as it offers the best views of lakes, mountains and glaciers in the region. The highway passes through some of the largest glaciers in the world including the Baltoro and Siachen Glaciers. And five of what is known as the 'eight-thousanders' of the world – mountains taller than 8,000 meters – are in Pakistan and accessible thanks to the highway.

But while the tourists come in their droves, travel on this highway is not for the faint of

heart. There are the most severe of hair pin bends to contend with, muddy streams to ford, and avalanches and landslides to dodge, often with little or no warning. The edge of the road is never very far from the tyres – and the edge of the road is truly the edge: there are no safety barriers on one side, and rock wall on the other. There is absolutely no room for error. Wheels often hang over the edge of the road, especially on the notoriously narrow and sharp bends, with a sheer drop off point thousands of meters above the valley below.

Many a car, bus and truck has driven too close to the edge and found themselves airborne and plunging into the valleys and rivers far beneath them. Many deaths have occurred and continue to do so due to the precarious height of the highway. Because of the sheer drop, many slow down to a snail's pace while traversing the road. As one

nervous driver said, 'It can take an hour to travel just one mile on the Karakoram, and only a second to depart it. It's hair-raising to say the least. It might be called the Eighth Wonder of the World, but we tend to call it the scariest road in the world.'

Burj Khalifa, World's Tallest Building
– Dubai, United Arab Emirates

The world's tallest building already has a rival and it's designed by the same architect.

It has been the world's tallest building since it soared to its final height of 829.8 metres (2,722 feet) in 2008.

The official name of this towering colossus is Burj Khalifa – meaning Burj Tower – but locals call it the Burj Dubai.

The funny thing is you don't look down in Dubai, you look up and marvel at this engineering wonder of reinforced concrete and gleaming glass.

It's risky calling this the world's tallest structure because, if history is anything to go by, no sooner has a building been declared the world's tallest than a crane can be seen on the horizon and the race to build a new 'tallest' is on once again.

At the moment work has already begun on Jeddah Tower. The tower is the brainchild of American architect, Adrian Smith. It was Adrian who gave us Burj Khalifa.

But Smith wants to go even higher. The Jeddah Tower, with its 167 floors, will be the first skyscraper to reach one kilometer in height. No longer called high-rise, this new breed of skyscraper is called a mega high-rise. The Jeddah will herald the arrival of the world's first mega-speedy elevator. As the buildings get taller, new technologies involving even faster lifts and the way these buildings are plumbed, air-conditioned and electrically fitted have to be developed. You don't want to be left taking the stairs in these massive buildings!

So while the Jeddah takes shape, (expected to become the world's tallest in 2020) – let's look at her current big brother, the Burj Khalifa.

The tower was conceived to herald Dubai's decision to shift from being an oil-based economy to a more tourism-focused market. And to do this they needed to put Dubai on the map with something truly eye-catching and sensational.

And along with it being the world's tallest building, the Burj Khalifa comes with very interesting construction facts.

>> DID YOU KNOW? <<

- The building was originally named Burj Dubai but was renamed to honor the ruler of Abu Dhabi and president of the United Arab Emirates (UAE), Khalifa bin Zayed Al Nahyan. Abu Dhabi and the UAE helped fund the project.

- More than 1,000 pieces of art adorn the interiors of Burj Khalifa.

- The spire of Burj Khalifa is composed of more than 4,000 tonnes of structural steel. The central pinnacle pipe weighs 350 tonnes and has a height of 200 meters (660) feet). The spire also houses communications equipment. They say the spire could be a skyscraper in its own right. It has been revealed without this unnecessary 'vanity' add-on, the Tower would be reduced from 828 meters to 585 meters.

- In high winds, the tower at its highest point sways a total of 1.5 meters (4.9 feet).

- The water system in the Burj Khalifa supplies an average of 946,000 liters of water per day through 100 kilometers of pipes. An additional 213 kilometers of piping serves the fire emergency system, and 34 kilometers of piping supplies chilled water for the building's air-conditioning system. The waste water system uses gravity to rid water from toilets, floor drains and rainstorms to the city's municipal sewer.

- To wash the 24,348 windows, totalling 120,000 square meters of glass, an automatic bucket system is in place to cover several levels. However, the top of the building is cleaned by a crew who use ropes to descend from the top to gain access. It takes 36 workers three to four months to clean the entire exterior façade.

- The Burj Khalifa is approximately three times the height of the Eiffel Tower and twice as tall as the Empire State Building.

- The building holds many records, including the tallest free-standing building in the world, highest occupied floor, the highest observation deck anywhere, and more storeys than any other building on the planet.

- It took more than 110,000 tons of concrete, 55,000 tons of steel and 22 million man-hours to complete the Burj Khalifa.

- If you laid all the steel used in the Burj Khalifa end to end it would stretch more than a quarter of the way around the world.

- There has been talk to build additional floors to the Burj Khalifa to keep it soaring as the world's tallest building.

- The building contains a total of 57 elevators and 8 escalators to keep people moving.

- The building of the structure was dogged with bad publicity concerning migrant workers from South Asia, who were the main labor force, being underpaid for their long hours of toil.

- Burj Khalifa boasts the world's highest outdoor observation deck: on the 124th floor at 452 meters (1,438 feet).

- The world's highest nightclub is on the 144th floor.

- The world's highest restaurant, At.Mosphere, can be found on the 122nd floor at a height of 442 meters (1,450 feet).

- It also stages the world's highest display of New Year fireworks.

- From the highest floors of the Burj, people can still see the sun for a couple of minutes after is has set on the ground. This has led Dubai clerics to rule that those living above the 80th floor have to wait two additional minutes to break their Ramadan fast, and those living above the 150th floor have to wait an extra three minutes.

The building has inspired and captured the imagination of the building and architecture industry all around the globe.

In June 2010, Burj Khalifa was voted Best Tall Building – Middle East & Africa, by the prestigious Council on Tall Buildings and Urban Habitat (the CTBUH).

CTBUH Awards Chair, Gordon Gill of Adrian Smith & Gordon Gill Architecture said: 'We are talking about a building here that has changed the landscape of what is possible in architecture a building that became internationally recognized as an icon long before it was even completed. "Building of the Century" was thought a more appropriate title for it.'

(Source: Wikipedia Burj Khalifa. www.thedailybeast.com/fun-facts-about-the-burj-khalifa-worlds-tallest-building-photos

The World's Longest Bridge and Other Bridge Wonders

The Danyang-Kunshan Grand Bridge – China.

Whether it be a Great Wall or a sprawling, record-breaking bridge – they like to do things big and long in China.

Although China has many engineering wonders to boast of, they are particularly proud of the Danyan-Kunshan Bridge, which has the honor of being the world's longest bridge. The bridge is a vital link in the Beijing-Shanghai high-speed railway.

Spanning 165 kilometers (102.5 miles), the elevated viaduct received the world's longest bridge title from the Guinness World Records when it opened in 2011.

It runs parallel to the great Yangtze River and passes stunning scenery including lowland rice paddies. It also crosses water like a traditional bridge should do; this part of the structure can be found in a 9 kilometer (5.6 mile) section, crossing the Yangcheng Lake in Suzhou.

Interestingly, on this very same rail line can be found the 113.6 kilometer (70.6 mile) Tianjin Grand Bridge, connecting Langfang to Qingxian, which has the honor of being the world's second-longest bridge.

Building of the Danyang-Kunshan Grand Bridge lasted four years, requiring an estimated 10,000 workers. The cost of the project blew out to a staggering US $8.5 billion.

Longest Continuous Bridge Over Water (troubled or otherwise).

LAKE PONTCHARTRAIN CAUSEWAY – LOUISIANA.

The good folk of Louisiana were outraged when Mr Guinness took the title of world's longest bridge away from them and gave it to the Chinese.

A compromise was met, with the Lake Pontchartrain Causeway being given the new title: the world's longest bridge running continuously over water.

The four-lane, 5,189-pile concrete trestle bridge is 38.41 kilometers (23.87 miles) long, and runs over open water for 38.3 kilometers (23.79 feet).

The bridge has also been listed as one of the 'world's scariest bridges', with CNN Travel describing it as 'a pulse-quickening half-hour drive'.

Source: www.livescience.com
www.historyofbridges.com/famous-bridges/longest-bridge-in-the-world/

CAPITAL GATE –
The Leaning Tower of
Abu Dhabi

She leans like one with the weight of the world on her shoulders. Her stoop is so pronounced she bends 18 degrees to the west.

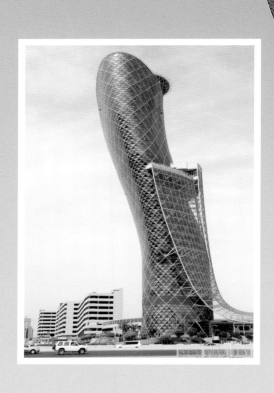

But this dazzling architectural wonder doesn't have a chip on her shoulder – she is just weighed down with countless awards, including the prestigious Guinness World Records honor of being the world's furthest-leaning man-made tower.

Eat your heart out Leaning Tower of Pisa!

Known as the Leaning Tower of Abu Dhabi, Capital Gate is an office building as well as housing a luxury hotel. It is possibly the most eye-catching building in Abu Dhabi – and Abu Dhabi has stacks of cutting edge, modern architecture at which to marvel.

Capital Gate stands at 160 meters tall (520 feet) and has 35 floors. The stunning tower is the focal point for the Capital Centre, the Abu Dhabi National Exhibition Centre master development.

The stunning structure regularly makes the list of being one of the ten most amazing Modern Architectural Wonders of the World.

Many are fearful of entering the leaning building; they approach with trepidation, not sure if it will topple over in the wind. Engineers assure the nervous that the building is rock solid and the gravitational pressure caused by the lean is countered with a revolutionary technique called pre-cambered core. This involves using a core of concrete reinforced with steel that is deliberately built slightly off-center.

The building is also anchored to the ground by 490 piles which are drilled 20–30 meters underground.

What is a 'pile' in construction?

Pile, in building construction, is a post-like foundation used from prehistoric times. In modern civil engineering, piles of timber, steel, or concrete are driven into the ground to support a structure; bridge piers may be supported on groups of large-diameter piles.

(Source) Pile | construction | Britannica.com
Source: www.oddee.com/item_99408.aspx
Wikipedia

The Theme Building, AKA 'That *Jetsons* Building' – Los Angeles International Airport, USA

This futuristic wonder, in a style known as mid-century modern architecture (or the more funky name, Googie) has influenced all devotees of late-50s and early-60s 'Space Age' design.

Just watch an episode of **The Jetsons** and you can see similar futuristic architecture. It was a trend that saw such buildings pop up all over LA in the mid-60s: airports, motels, fast food joints, and houses all went space-y. The modern architects just couldn't get enough of this look that was 'Googie', or simply out of this world.

What Is Googie?

Googie is a form of modern architecture, a subdivision of futurist architecture influenced by car culture, jets, the Space Age and the Atomic Age. It originated in Southern California in the late 1940s, continuing approximately into the mid-1960s. You could find it in motels, coffee houses and gas stations. The style later became known as part of the mid-century modern style. The term 'Googie' comes from a now-defunct café in West Hollywood designed by John Lautner, a student of modern architecture legend and hero, Frank Lloyd Wright.

Features of Googie include upswept roofs, curvaceous geometric shapes and bold use of glass, steel and neon (think the famous Las Vegas sign). The Las Vegas of the 1950s was one of the first large-scale experiments in Googie architecture. The Las Vegas sign embodied the futuristic style with the signature starburst and bold colors. It said future and fun at the same time.

If built, many of the buildings in *The Jetsons* would be considered Googie.

Googie can be recognized by Space Age designs symbolic of motion, such as boomerangs, flying saucers, diagrammatic atoms and parabolas, and free-form designs such as 'soft' parallelograms and an 'artist's palette' motif. These classic Googie symbols represented America's fascination with Space Age themes and marketing emphasis on futuristic designs. As with the Art Deco style of the 1930s, Googie became less valued as time passed, and many buildings in this style have been destroyed. Some examples have been preserved, such as the oldest McDonald's (located in Downey, California), and the Los Angeles International Airport Theme Building.

(Source: Googie Architecture Wikipedia, Architectural Digest 5 of the Best Googie Buildings in LA).

Cartoon Constructions.

You see the iconic Theme Building the moment you arrive at Los Angeles International Airport. It looms there resembling a 1960s flying saucer that has just landed on its four legs.

Downey McDonald's.

The famous Las Vegas sign.

The gorgeously Googie Seattle Space Needle.

Disney's Tomorrowland is a Space Age fantasy.

Its groovy, Space Age architecture instantly conjures cartoon classic **The Jetsons** or **The Thunderbirds** show. For the time, this building was as futuristic and Space Age as you could get.

The Theme Building has been wowing the world since 1961. A year later, **The Jetsons** – featuring a futuristic all-American family zipping around in flying saucers – had clearly been influenced by the prophetic design of the Theme Building.

All buildings in **The Jetsons** futuristic animated landscape clearly resembled the Theme Building.

That is hardly surprising as the artists and animators working on **The Jetsons** didn't have to go far to find inspiration. The Hanna-Barbera Studio was nestled in Hollywood and in the 1950s and early 1960s this was heartland for buildings that had that mid-20th century modern look that would be called 'Jetsonian' and later, Googie.

The people behind designing **The Jetsons** look could find instant inspiration at Disney's Tomorrowland in Anaheim, countless Googie coffee shops in Southern California, and of course at the most iconic Googie building in

the world – the Theme Building at the Los Angeles International Airport.

It has been said that during the 1962–63 seasons of **The Jetsons**, LA was so dripping with Googie architecture it could be argued Hanna-Barbera animators didn't really exaggerate the style – they copied it. How could they not? They were surrounded by it.

The most fantastic part of the Theme Building was the Googie-style Encounter Restaurant. A quick elevator ride up into the spaceship-like structure would see you plunged into a very funky Googie heaven.

Encounter opened in 1997 and it was the design brainchild of Ed Sotto and Ellen Guevara of Walt Disney's Imagineering team. Together they grabbed the retro/futuristic inspired Googie ball and ran with it. It fit the style so well that it looked like it had been there since the building was first opened.

Sadly, despite its many fans, the Encounter Restaurant closed unexpectedly in December 2013. And like some treasure, buried in a time capsule, it remains suspended in time with no current plans to re-open it.

Thankfully the observation deck in the Theme Building is still open from 8 a.m. to 5 p.m. Saturdays and Sundays. The building, declared an LA cultural and historical building in 1992, was designed by Paul R. Williams, Pereira & Luckman and Robert Herrick Carter. It still looms ready to take off like the 'Jetsonian' flying saucer it resembles. Hopefully the Encounter Restaurant will one day also come along for the ride.

Other Fantastic Googie Structures:

Downey McDonald's: You will want to stop for a thickshake and fries at this downtown McDonald's. Built in 1953 in Downey LA, it is the oldest McDonald's in the world. The building is pure Googie with the famous Golden Arches incorporated into the building's iconic structure.

Union 76 Station: Yes, it's a petrol station, but the Union 76 Station in Beverly Hills is one of the finest examples of Googie architecture. Designed by Gin Wong, the building has its trademark boomerang-shaped roof and modern, clean lines. But most of all – it's fun. You wouldn't be surprised if George Jetson turned up at the pump to fill up his flying saucer.

Pann's Restaurant: The classic lines of the roof and typically Googie sign gets you in straight away.

Space Needle: Googie style didn't just hang around LA. It moved north and found a strong base in Seattle. Googie buildings abounded in Seattle and the city's most famous icon, the Space Needle (a giant, hovering flying saucer), is probably the best homage to the style there is.

The Las Vegas Sign: This iconic Googie sign says 'future' and 'fun' at the same time. The Las Vegas of the 1950s was one of the first large-scale experiments in Googie architecture. The Las Vegas sign embodied the futuristic style with the signature starburst and bold colors. The sign is timeless and when people conjure a mental picture of Vegas, they usually see the sign.

The Monsanto 'House Of The Future'.

Once a huge attraction at Disneyland California's Tomorrowland, the Monsanto House of the Future drew huge crowds between 1957 and 1967.

The 1,200 square meter house was created by Monsanto, Massachusetts Institute of Technology, and Walt Disney Imagineering. The house had been imagined to look like a home from the year 1986. It was eerily accurate in many ways – featuring household appliances such as microwaves and dishwashers that would eventually become the norm in everyday homes...except they hadn't actually been invented yet.

Suspended seemingly in mid-air on a 1.5 square meter block of concrete, the plastic and fibreglass structure wowed more than 20 million visitors who flocked to see the way of the future.

Fans of the Googie-type House of the Future have asked for the House to be returned to Disneyland as it is a perfect example of the architecture. It is believed the House is in a secret storage area of Disneyland and may well soon be on display again in the not-too-distant future.

Sources: Architectural Digest.
Smithsonianmag.com.
Wikipedia
Offbeat LA
Googie Architecture: Futurism Through Modernism

And in the Future...
DUBAI'S DYNAMIC TOWER HOTEL

The future in architecture looks very exciting and is bound to have us all in a spin with the incredible Rotating Tower of Dubai.

Known as the Dynamic Tower, it is truly dynamic by name, by design and by nature.

There has been no structure like it. The Dynamic Tower, also known as the Dynamic Architecture Building or the Da Vinci Tower, is planned to be offering exciting twists and turns in the Dubai skyline by 2020.

Plans for the Dynamic began in 2008. It will be a building constantly in motion. It will change its shape regularly, never appearing the same way twice. Talk about a building with endless combinations and variety.

The brainchild of architect Dr David Fisher, of the Dynamic Group, this flexible, ever-changing building covering 80 floors and soaring to just over 420 meters (1,378 feet) is expected to cost United Arab Emirates Dirham (AED) 2 billion or over half a billion USD.

The central tower will allow each floor to move independently. One floor will be able to fully rotate around the tower over three hours. Residents will have the choice of waking up to sunrise and enjoying sunsets over the ocean at dinner.

The Dynamic will be the world's first prefabricated skyscraper. Each floor will be constructed in a factory and shipped over to the yet-to-be decided site. The Dynamic Group are aiming to build each floor in six days.

The building will be a mix of private apartments and hotel accommodation. Voice-activation technology will allow the floors to move at the owner or visitor's request.

Dynamic will be powered from wind turbines and solar panels. It is anticipated that enough surplus electricity should be produced to power five other similar sized buildings in the vicinity. The turbines will be placed between each of the rotating floors. Apart from being a fully functioning building, it will also be a true green power plant.

The structure will look more like a sculpture, a piece of precious art rather than a run-of-the-mill glass skyscraper. By the time it is completed, it will become the second-tallest building in Dubai.

This revolutionary, revolving structure goes way beyond dynamic. It will be the ultimate building of the future.

First published in 2018 by New Holland Publishers
London • Sydney • Auckland

131-151 Great Titchfield Street, London W1W 5BB, United Kingdom
1/66 Gibbes Street, Chatswood, NSW 2067, Australia
5/39 Woodside Ave, Northcote, Auckland 0627, New Zealand

newhollandpublishers.com

A record of this book is held at the British Library and the National Library of Australia.

ISBN 9781921580499

Group Managing Director: Fiona Schultz
Publisher: Monique Butterworth
Project Editor: Rebecca Sutherland
Designer: Sara Lindberg
Production Director: James Mills-Hicks
Printer: Toppan Leefung Printing Limited, China

10 9 8 7 6 5 4 3 2 1

Keep up with New Holland Publishers on Facebook
facebook.com/NewHollandPublishers